SEO Step-by-Step

The Complete Beginner's Guide to Getting Traffic from Google

D0359351

By Caimin Jones,
best-selling author of

WordPress Websites Step-by-Step
The Complete Beginner's Guide to Building
a Website

ISBN: 978-1497415027

Praise for this book

"Simply written and very straightforward. Highly recommended."

Christine F. Anderson

"I love this book because finally I have a clear, concise, yet comprehensive guide to search engine optimization (SEO). The guide is completely up-to-date, which is critical because search algorithms change often. I highly recommend this book for beginners."

A. Stowe

"If you are ready to learn about SEO or you want to make your site more attractive to Google and Bing, this book provides great knowledge and resources. Recommended."

Gerardo A. Dada - Marketer, technologist, theadaptivemarketer.com

Contents

Welcome

Thank you for buying this book. My name is Caimin and I've been building websites for myself and clients since 1998. This guide is inspired by the problems I've seen people run into when trying to get traffic to their website.

This book is written for the complete SEO beginner in plain English, focusing on strategies anyone can follow and that won't get you banned from Google. If you can write a blog post or a web page, I can show you how to get traffic to it.

Because this is a beginner's guide, it's been proofread many times to make sure it's the easiest guide possible. That said, if there's anything you're still not clear about, please feel free to email me and I'll try to help. My email address is on the last page of this book.

That's also where you'll find a special link that'll get you a free, no-obligation two-week trial of SEMRush.com - one of the best premium SEO tools out there. You don't need to use it to start getting more traffic to your site, it's just a little gift I arranged as a thank you for buying this book.

If you've poured your heart and soul into creating content for a website or blog - only to find it doesn't get the traffic it deserves - you're not alone.

Getting visitors to your site isn't always easy. You probably know you need to learn SEO but the trouble is there are so many SEO "gurus" slithering around you'd be forgiven for thinking it was a mysterious black art that takes years to learn, or can only be mastered by an elite group with insider knowledge.

But the truth is, the fundamentals of SEO are straightforward. You can learn them and start seeing increased visits to your website within a week.

The first step is to understand that the goal of search engines is to keep users coming back by consistently delivering useful search results. They do that by investing millions every year in programming algorithms that try to predict as accurately as possible which content users will find most useful.

Everything they do revolves around that one objective. Once you understand that, you know the golden rule of getting traffic - whether from search engines, social media or content marketing:

Create content real people love - on subjects they're searching for - and search engine traffic will follow.

If you follow that rule, you'll attract users who will:

• Stay on your site longer
• Look at more pages
• Come back to your site again and again
• Tweet, Like, and share your content

These actions are signals that Google and other search engines measure and use as quality indicators when deciding how high sites and pages should rank. The more users you have on your site taking one or more of the above actions, the higher you will rank.

How search engines work

Here are the three main steps search engines use to decide which content should be promoted to the top of search results.

1. They visit your site to create an index of the content to understand what individual pages are about, as well as the overall subject of your site.

2. They count the links from other sites and blogs as "votes" on the quality of the content.

3. They count social shares - likes, tweets, etc. - as more "votes" on your content.

Although search engine algorithms are a complex mix of hundreds of ranking factors, most aspects of search engine optimization fit in to one of these areas.

That's why this book concentrates on those three areas. By the end of the book, you'll be an expert in on-page SEO, link-building and getting the maximum amount of social shares for each piece of content you publish.

"White-hat" SEO vs. "Black-hat" SEO

There are two types of SEO. This book is about White-hat SEO. It uses the honest tips and techniques I've used to increase the rankings of my sites and those of my clients over the last sixteen years.

Black-hat SEO, on the other hand, uses tricks and loopholes to try to game the system and trick search engines into ranking a site as high as possible, regardless of the quality of the content.

I'm sure you've seen ads promising a shortcut to page one of Google. Just buy Product X, adjust a few settings and wait a few days for a torrent of traffic. At worst, products like those are scams. At best, they're software that exploits a loophole.

The problem with loopholes is that sooner or later, Google closes the loophole.

Not so long ago, an easy way to improve rankings was to write a single article and then use software called an article spinner to create and submit slight variations of it to hundreds of different article directories. Within the content of the articles would be links back to the webmasters site - generating hundred of backlinks in a short time, leading to better rankings.

Just one problem.

Overnight Google changed its algorithm. Not only did it downgrade almost all article directories to junk status, it kicked sites using the article spinning trick out of its search results.

This meant improved search results for users, but a lot of black-hat SEO "engineers" having to undo years of work in an attempt to repair their rankings.

That's why I recommend sticking to white-hat SEO techniques - they work and they're a reliable long-term strategy.

Let's get started!

STEP 1
Choose The Right
Keywords For Your Niche

Choosing the Right Keywords

Great content is essential for a successful website, but if you write posts on subjects nobody searches for, you'll never get any real search engine traffic.

That's why a smart search engine optimization strategy begins with choosing the best keywords - there's no point being on page one for a search term that nobody uses.

Good keyword phrases have two essential qualities:

1. Significant number of monthly searches
(plenty of search engine traffic)

2. Low competition
(not so many existing search results for the terms that it will be difficult - or impossible - to rank highly for the term)

Many people struggle with getting traffic to their site because they haven't researched their keywords correctly. Instead, they just guess.

Here's an example of how guessing can lead you astray. Take these three keyword phrases:

cooking
cooking games
cooking recipes

All are popular search terms, but the one with the largest search volume has over sixteen times more people using it each month than the next most popular.

Which one is it? I don't know about you, but my guess would be "cooking". But at the time of writing, these were the actual numbers of people searching for each term every month on Google.

cooking 135,000
cooking recipes 49,500
cooking games 2,240,000

That's why it's important to spend time researching keywords - it's often hard to guess what the most popular search terms are.

Guessing incorrectly means you waste time and energy targeting keywords that have low search volume and so never bring you many visitors, even if you rank highly for them.

Your secret keyword tool

There are a number of keyword research tools, but the most accurate and easy to use is the Google Keyword Planner.

Important: You may have seen out-of-date guides recommend a different tool called the Google AdWords Keyword Tool. The Keyword Planner replaces the AdWords Tool, which is no longer available.

The Keyword Planner is a free tool designed to help advertisers choose keywords when buying ads on AdSense, Google's advertising network. You can use the same information to discover the best keywords to target in your niche. Not just keywords you think people use, but the ones they really do.

You'll find the Keywords Planner at:
http://adwords.google.com/keywordplanner

Because the Keyword Planner is only available to logged in users, you'll need to create an AdWords account to use it. It's free and you can use the same account as the one you may already have for other Google services likes Gmail and AdSense. You don't have to actually run an ad campaign to use the planner.

To find out more about creating an AdWords account, take a look at this link: *https://support.google.com/adwords/answer/1704354*

Using the Keyword Planner

When the Keyword Planner opens, you'll see a screen with a number of choices. Choose the option that says *Search for a new keyword and ad group ideas*, then type the keywords you want to check in the box labeled *Your product or service.*

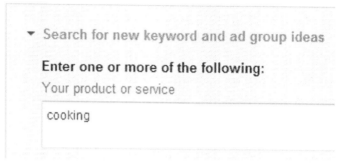

There are a lot of other options on the page, but there's only one that you need to edit. Click the panel that says *Keyword Options.*

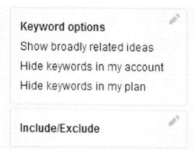

Then set *Only show ideas closely related to my search terms* to *On.* This setting will stop the suggestions list from becoming too large and unfocused to be useful.

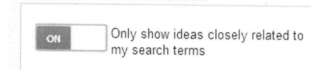

To generate your keyword suggestion list, click the *Get Ideas* button. On the results page you'll notice two tabs - *Ad Groups* and *Keyword Ideas.* For our purposes, *Ad Groups* isn't too helpful, so click the *Keyword Ideas* tab.

You'll see your keyword phrase at the top, with a second table under listing similar keywords. By default this table is ordered alphabetically by keyword, which makes it harder to see which keywords have the most traffic. Clicking the *Avg. monthly searches* heading will reorder the table so that it shows keywords by search volume from highest to lowest.

You now have a list of search phrases related to your keyword with the most popular searches at the top.

<u>Tip</u>: If your keyword search isn't turning up enough results to be useful - or you want to try a different search term - click the *Modify Search* button and change the keywords under *Your product or service*.

What the keyword table tells you

Once you know how to read it, the second table can tell you exactly which keywords will be the most profitable in a particular niche. For keyword research, the only columns we need to consider are *Avg. monthly searches* and *Suggested bid*.

Ad group ideas	Keyword ideas
Search Terms	
cooking	

Avg. monthly searches
This column lists the average number of Google searches for each keyword every month, based on the preceding twelve months of data. A dash (-) instead of number indicates "insufficient data", meaning there are so few searches each month there's no sense concentrating on that keyword.

Suggested bid
This is useful if you're using AdSense or other advertising on your site, doing affiliate marketing, or selling your own product. Keywords with high suggested bids indicate a phrase where the user is said to have "commercial intent".

These are phrases used by people who are further along the buying process than the average user. They're typically only one or two steps away from buying a product, which is why advertisers will pay more to reach them - they're easier to make a sale from.

For example, at the time of writing, "phone" has a much lower *Suggested Bid* than the phrase "cell phone plans". The second phrase is a money keyword (with "commercial intent") because it's clear the user is only a step or two from buying a specific product.

When you successfully rank for phrases like these, you'll be attracting visitors ready to click ads, affiliate links or buy products. If you're running AdSense, you'll also be attracting advertisers paying the kind of high payments you see listed under Suggested Bid.

Putting it all together: Creating a list of the most profitable keywords in your niche

For each potential keyword, we need to know three things:

1. Are there enough people searching for the phrase to generate worthwhile traffic?

2. How easy will it be to compete with the pages already being listed for that keyword?

3. Is it a "money" keyword?

Imagine I have a blog about arts and crafts and I'm looking for post ideas about scrapbooking. It's a popular subject, but how popular?

Running the keyword through Keyword Planner gives me the search volume but I also need to know the search competition - how many pages Google already has for that term. The fewer there are, the easier it will be for my page to appear near the top of Google results for that phrase.

AdWords doesn't include this information, so you'll need to do a quick Google search and note the number of results listed at the top of the page.

Here's the combined information from AdWords and Google search results for scrapbooking:

scrapbooking
Avg. monthly searches: 165,000, Suggested bid: $0.41, Google Results: 44,800,000

scrapbooking ideas
Avg. monthly searches: 14,800, Suggested bid: $0.88, Google Results: 33,400,000

scrapbooking supplies
Avg. monthly searches: 14,800, Suggested bid: $0.61, Google Results: 13,200,000

digital scrapbooking
Avg. monthly searches: 12,100, Suggested bid: $1.58, Google Results: 14,200,000

scrapbooking paper
Avg. monthly searches: 4,400, Suggested bid: $0.46, Google Results: 43,200,000

scrapbooking layouts
Avg. monthly searches: 4,400, Suggested bid: $0.49, Google Results: 4,510,000

Note: *Suggested bid* is a guide to how much AdWords advertisers need to pay for their ads to appear for that term.

What's clear is that *scrapbooking* is a good term for SEO. The main keyword, *scrapbooking*, is popular (165,000 searches per month) but the number of search results (44,800,000) is not that high. In other words, there are lots of people searching for the term but not that much competition from other sites. That's exactly the kind of keyword we're looking for.

How Search Volume translates to visitors

As a rough guide, the top result on page one for any search query will get monthly visits equal to around 40% of the search volume listed in

AdWords, while the tenth result on page one will get 2% of the volume. Here's how every position from 1 to 10 stacks up:

1 - 36.4%
2 - 12.5%
3 - 9.5%
4 - 7.9%
5 - 6.1%
6 - 4.1%
7 - 3.8%
8 - 3.5%
9 - 3.0%
10 - 2.2%

[source: http://searchenginewatch.com/]

For the term *scrapbooking*, that translates to around 66,000 visits for the first results and 3,300 visits per month for the tenth result. It's clear that even sites on the second page of results for this keyword should be getting a couple of thousand clicks a month.

To sum up, look for keywords that relate to your niche and have at least two of the following qualities:

1. High search volume
2. Low competition
3. High *Suggested bid*

If you find a keyword with all three, you've definitely found a "money topic".

Targeting Long Tail Keywords

A *long tail keyword* is a phrase of three or more words which is related to your main keywords but has less traffic associated with it.

Why would you want to target phrases with less traffic?

Most content creators go for the big, obvious one and two keyword phrases and ignore these longer search phrases. Thankfully, less competition means fewer pages in the results, making it easier for you to rank highly.

Take a look at the Google Keyword Planner and you'll see that many long tail keywords attract a good amount of traffic.

For example, at the time of writing, *photography* has 450,000 monthly searches with over one and a half billion search results, making it an impossibly difficult keyword to target successfully.

However, the long tail phrase *tilt shift photography* has a respectable 10,000 searches a month but only three million pages in the results. That means a good, in-depth post on the subject with only a handful of links to it should rank well for that term.

When considering your overall keyword strategy, don't forget long-tail keywords. For many established websites (including the sites I run) the combined number of visits from long-tail keywords is greater than those generated by the main keywords.

That's not surprising, given that long tail keywords account for 70% of all search engine queries. But there's another benefit to creating content with the long tail in mind - those queries tend to be used by people about to buy. Someone searching for phones is just browsing, while someone searching for Apple iPhone best price probably has their credit card out already.

That means if you're selling products or doing affiliate marketing you should definitely be targeting long tail keywords. If you're generating revenue with AdSense, you'll often find visitors who find your site via long tail searches are more likely to click ads as they continue searching for the best deal.

Even if you're not monetizing your site, the long tail can provide your site with a lot of targeted, motivated readers - the kind that share your links and sign up for your email updates.

STEP 2
Create Great Content

How to Write Content Google Loves

"In general, webmasters can improve the rank of their sites by creating high-quality sites that users will want to use and share."

The quote above, taken from Google's Webmaster Guidelines, makes it clear how important site content now is for SEO. At the heart of a site that works for both search engines and visitors is great content. Without that, no amount of SEO or social media marketing will help.

What is great content?

Successful sites consistently produce content that is:

Readable
Usable
Shareable

Let's look at those three things in more detail.

Readable

Not only does your content have to be something people will <u>want</u> to read, it has to be <u>easy</u> to read.

Good ways to boost readability include breaking up sub-topics within your post, using images and videos to help explain difficult concepts, and visually highlighting one or two quotable "sound bites" that illustrate key points.

Avoid long, dense sentences and paragraphs. Short and punchy works best.

Usable

Most visitors need information.

Check forums, online communities and Q&A sites to find the questions people in your niche are asking. Providing clear answers with actionable points is a sure-fire way of creating content your target audience will love.

It's also a highly effective SEO strategy. When you think about it, search engine queries are really questions - and if people are asking something on a forum, they're also asking it on Google.

Provide comprehensive, accurate answers and you'll rank highly.

Shareable

Getting content shared through social networks is vital for SEO.

As well as being original and well-written, the posts that get shared the most also have a killer headline (one that's challenging, thought-provoking, shocking, funny, or intriguing), and a striking, relevant image.

Page Titles and Keywords

The title you give your post is the single most important element of on-page SEO.

Not only do pages with keywords in the title rank better, taking the time to write a great title will make the difference between a moderate click-through rate and a great one.

The reason is simple. The title is the first thing users see in search results:

5 **Writing Tips** to Jumpstart Your Business **Blog** | Social Media Tc
socialmediatoday.com/.../5-**writing-tips**-jumpstart-your-business-**blog** ▾
Nov 14, 2013 - These 5 **writing tips** to get your business **blog** started will help
on the path to creating a strong Web Presence for your business.

In fact, aside from the text snippet underneath, it's pretty much the only thing users can see - meaning page titles have a huge influence on whether a link is clicked.

Make sure every page or post you publish has a title that:

1. Has relevant keywords so it shows up in the right search results

2. Tempts users to click the link to your site

The example above, *5 Writing Tips to Jumpstart Your Business Blog*, is a great example. It has the keywords blog writing tips and also sounds inviting by promising five nuggets of info that could have a big impact on a blog.

One of the best places to see compelling headlines in action is the content marketing blog Copyblogger.com. Take a look at the example headlines below - all taken from Copyblogger posts - and notice how each has both a clear subject and practically begs you to click it.

11 Common Blogging Mistakes That Are Wasting Your Audience's Time

The 5 Things Every (Great) Marketing Story Needs

How to Write Interesting Content for a "Boring" Topic

7 Scientifically-Backed Copywriting Tips

Seven Ways Writers Can Build Online Authority with Google+

9 Persuasion Lessons from a 4-Year-Old

The 5 Most Persuasive Words in the English Language

10 Steps to a Secure WordPress Website

22 Ways to Create Compelling Content When You Don't Have a Clue

Remember to be punchy and concise - you don't have unlimited space for your title. Search engines allow 65-75 characters before cutting off a title.

without images.

For best results, use images related to the subject that are truly striking, funny or beautiful. Be sure to check the image still looks good even when reduced to thumbnail size.

Remember that you don't have to use a photo - a good illustration can be equally effective.

When you share a link on Google+ or Facebook, the update form automatically includes images published in the post. If you don't see the correct image in the preview of the update, click the arrows near the image preview to select which image is used.

If your site uses a lot of imagery, consider adding a *Pin It* button to allow Pinterest users to easily add images to their boards. For sites with lots of high-quality product, inspirational or instructional images, Pinterest can be a major driver of traffic - especially given that every Pin and Repin of your image will include a link back to your site.

Finding good images

One of the best places to find images that are free to use is the Creative Commons section of Flickr:

http://www.flickr.com/creativecommons

A link back is a condition of use for most Creative Commons photos, so you need to make sure you include it with the image or at the end of the post.

You can also use this as a way of getting extra links by visiting the Flickr photo page and adding a comment thanking the photographer for the image, including a link where they can see their image in use.

As well as generating a link to your site, it's an extra courtesy that many photographers appreciate.

Creating Viral Infographics Without Design Skills

If you ever doubted we're living in a visual age, the continued popularity of the infographic should put you straight. It seems you can't login to a social network without seeing at least one link to an infographic that's doing the rounds.

Infographics are like blog posts - some are lame beyond belief but good ones bring a ton of traffic to the creators and are worth every bit of the time taken to create them.

If you're an artist or designer you can probably whip one up over your morning coffee. But even those of us lacking graphic design skills can still rustle up a decent looking infographic using one of the web apps listed below.

It's as simple as selecting a template and adding the data, facts and headings you want the infographic to cover.

The sources you use for your data will depend on your site niche, but associations and non-profit organizations are usually a good start. The more surprising the figures the more attention your infographic is likely to get.

Don't forget you can combine facts from a number of different sources into a single infographic.

If you're really stuck for an idea, take a look at the big blogs that cover your topic for mentions of recent surveys and studies.

Make sure you credit data sources at the bottom of the infographic. You'll also want to add a Created by... credit with your web address. Many of the services below also allow you to create an embeddable version, making it easier for people to be able to share the infographic and link back to your site.

Free web apps for creating infographics

http://www.creately.com
http://www.infogr.am
http://piktochart.com/
http://www.visual.ly

Resource Lists

Creating a truly indispensable resource list takes a lot of time. But a good one will generate lots of links and social activity, bringing you a lot of traffic for years to come.

Take a look at these examples, with the number of inbound links they had at the time of writing:

50 Ideas on Using Twitter for Business
http://www.chrisbrogan.com/50-ideas-on-using-twitter-for-business/
54,404 links

Blogging Tips for Beginners
http://www.problogger.net/archives/2006/02/14/blogging-for-beginners-2/
1,510,000 links

How to Write Magnetic Headlines
http://www.copyblogger.com/magnetic-headlines/
168,000 links

Those are some pretty good numbers.

Copyblogger in particular is crammed full of posts that have a lot social shares, links and SEO success.

Indispensable resources usually take the form of either a list post or an in-depth how-to.

Creating a list post

The key to a successful list post is no more complicated than including a large number of quality items. If you publish a post called the *5 Best Photographers Ever* it'll be forgotten in no time. But create an epic called the *100 Best Portrait, Landscape, Architectural and Street*

Photographers of All Time, featuring twenty-five of each type of photographer with links, a bio and examples of their work and you'll have a fascinating resource readers will love.

List posts don't have to be based on links. A post like *101 Tips for Self-Published Authors* would also do well - provided each tip was useful, well-thought out and actionable.

In-depth how-to posts

Take an aspect of your niche that people find difficult and create the most comprehensive tutorial there is on the subject. This could be an advanced topic or a fundamental skill that needs to be mastered before you can really become proficient at something.

Include step-by-step instructions and walk the reader through the entire process. Use images and videos if they make the concept or skill you're teaching clearer.

As with list posts, the aim is to come up with an absolutely compelling go-to resource.

Top 50 Lists

Creating a list of the top 10, 20 or 50 most powerful or influential blogs and websites in your niche creates plenty of room for discussion, debate and controversy - not to mention links as other bloggers write posts telling you you've got it wrong, or who you've missed out.

Once your list starts gaining a bit of traction and fame, you'll find the people listed will naturally start mentioning and linking to you because everyone likes to brag a little now and then. You might want to create a I'm in the Top 20 Power List of... badge to let people boast a bit more. To kick-start things after publishing your first list, contact everyone listed to let them know the link and why they're on the list.

How to choose who goes on the list

That's up to you. It could be straight science - number of Facebook Likes, Twitter followers, etc. Or it could be more subjective, looking at things like influence or quality of content.

If you're looking to stir up a bit of controversy - never a bad thing if you want to generate links and traffic - then you can decide the list based on nothing more than your own opinion.

Don't forget the list will need to be updated regularly (probably monthly or quarterly) to keep it interesting and in people's minds.

Product lists

You can use this same technique for products related to your niche. By combining reviews with the Amazon Best Sellers list for the corresponding category, you can create a definitive list of the current best cameras, kitchen gadgets, or other products related to your niche.

Use an Amazon affiliate link for each product and you've also got yourself an extra income stream.

STEP 3
Optimize Your Site

Keyword Placement & Density

Keywords and their placement are one of the most blogged about aspects of SEO. But the reality is that for modern day SEO, there are only two things to think about:

1. Am I using too many keywords?
2. Am I using too few keywords?

The rule for post titles is easy - use keyword phrase only once.

For the actual content, it's a little more complicated.

Keyword density is the percentage of words in your content that form a keyword phrase. Most SEO experts agree that the best keyword density is between 1 and 2 percent.

That means that in an article of 600 words, somewhere between 6 and 12 words should be part of a keyword phrase.

More than that makes content appear spammy, less and it may be difficult for search engines to accurately pick up what the content is about and you may not rank for some phrases.

In most cases, just writing in a natural way will give you the kind of keyword density you need. That said, it's a good idea to check to make sure your keyword density falls within the range above.

There are a number of online tools for doing this, one of the best lets you either paste in text or load a url:
http://tools.seobook.com/general/keyword-density/

If you're a WordPress user, take a look at this plugin which checks content before publishing:
http://wordpress.org/plugins/wordpress-seo/

Internal and External Linking Strategies

When it comes to SEO, there are two types of links - internal and external.

Internal links

Any link to another part of the same site is called an internal link. As well as links you'd expect to find - within a menu bar, for example - you can also create internal links by linking to past posts within newer ones.

This is known to be a thing Google likes, so get into the habit of including links to related posts. That also has the bonus of drawing readers deeper into your site by showing them links to pages they wouldn't otherwise have visited. Don't go overboard with your internal linking or you risk overwhelming the reader. One or two relevant links per post is usually a good maximum, more in longer posts.

It's important to remember that only straight HTML links count for SEO purposes. Links inside Flash files, Javascript or in form elements like dropdown menus can't be reliably followed by search engine spiders, so won't help your SEO.

External links

Google loves good quality content that links to other good quality content, so don't be afraid to include a link to another site if:

- It's a post that inspired you to write yours

- It's an authority post or blog in your niche

- It's a post you think deserves to be read and relates to your topic

Linking out to other reputable sites in your niche is a strategy that works - and not just because Google likes it.

Most bloggers check their site stats regularly and notice when a new site starts sending them traffic. Often, they'll pay a visit out of curiosity and will try to find a way to repay you either by leaving a comment or by linking back to you.

This happens a lot more than you might imagine, especially if you link to more than just the big sites in your niche. Smaller sites are usually one-person operations, so it's much easier to come to the attention of the content writer and bag yourself a mention, a link and hopefully an ongoing relationship with a like-minded blogger.

Using "nofollow" correctly

Originally devised as a way to combat comment spam, when a *nofollow* attribute is added to a link it tells search engines that your link to it isn't necessarily a "vote of confidence".

Situations where you'd want to use *nofollow* include:

- Affiliate, banner and other paid links

- Links where you can't vouch for the content, like links in user comments

- Pages on your own site that have no useful content like registration or login pages

Links with the *nofollow* attribute follow this format:

```
<a href="/login/" rel="nofollow">Login</a>
```

Too many *nofollow* links can be interpreted as an attempt to manipulate rankings (an outdated tactic called "link sculpting"), so be careful not to overdo it.

Claiming Your AuthorRank with Google

When it launched, Google revolutionized search by introducing PageRank - a measure of how reputable a page is based on the number and quality of other pages that link to it.

Now it seems as though Google is launching a similar measurement for the author of pages, called *AuthorRank*.

I say "it seems", because Google hasn't yet made any official announcement about *AuthorRank*. That said, most SEO experts agree it's coming and will have an impact on Google rankings. The nearest thing to an official announcement so far as has been a comment by Eric Schmidt, executive chairman of Google, in his recent book called *The Digital Age*. In it, Schmidt says:

Within search results, information tied to verified online profiles will be ranked higher than content without such verification, which will result in most users naturally clicking on the top (verified) results. The true cost of remaining anonymous, then, might be irrelevance.

It's clear that some kind of *AuthorRank* will become crucial for SEO in the future, especially since Google already offers verified profiles in the form of Google+ profiles and a content author tag.

No matter what happens in the future, there are already huge benefits to author identification. The most obvious is the author profile photo Google shows in search results.

20 Quick **Tips** on **Writing** Great **Blog** Posts : @ProBlogger

www.**problogger**.net/archives/2013/.../**writing**-great-**blog**-posts/
by Darren Rowse - in 151,483 Google+ circles
Aug 8, 2013 - In preparation for an interview on **writing** great **blog** cont
jotted down some 'quick **tips**'. While they are all ...

Studies show users click results with author pictures much more than results without images. One study carried out by the marketing company Catalyst discovered the increase in click-through can be as much as 150%. That means having your picture next to your result will bring more traffic even if your actual ranking stays the same. In fact, because our eyes are drawn to human faces, a page appearing at number 8 or 9 in the search results with a picture often attracts as many clicks as higher ranking pages.

Setting up a verified profile

Becoming a verified author is a two-step process. The first is to create a Google+ profile that serves as your identification, the second is to tell Google which sites you write content for. There are a number of ways to complete this process - including using the html tag *rel="author"* - but the method here is the one recommended by Google. It's also the easiest and doesn't involve making edits to HTML files which might get lost if you change your site around.

The first thing you need is a Google+ profile. If you don't already have one, create one here: *https://plus.google.com*

Unlike many social networks, Google+ gives you lots of space to write an in-depth profile. Your profile page will be prominently displayed in search results when people search for you by name, so it's worth taking the time to write a detailed profile.

Add a high-quality image of yourself. This is the image that will appear in Google search results next to pages you've authored, so check it still looks good when reduced to around 45 pixels in size.

Next, go to the *Contributor* to section of your profile and add the URL of every website you write create content for.

The final step is to make sure that on each of those sites you have:

- A recognizable profile picture (ideally the same one used for your Google+ profile)

- A byline with the same name as your Google+ profile

• An email address on the same domain

Once all three are in place, go to the link below to add the email address to your profile (you can prevent it being made public if you wish): *https://plus.google.com/authorship*

The email address is needed to verify that you really do write for that website. If you don't have one on that domain, you can use an alternative method to verify your identity - you'll find more info on the page above.

The final step is to wait a while.

It can take around two or three weeks for your profile photo to start appearing in relevant search results, though it's often sooner.

In the meantime, you can preview how your new search results will look here: *http://www.google.com/webmasters/tools/richsnippets*

SEO-friendly URLs

A well-optimized URL is one that isn't too long and contains 2-5 words describing the content. It looks something like this:

www.somesite.com/windows-8-help/

Search engines (and users) prefer URLs like the above to ones that look like this:

www.somesite.com/trkr.cgi?ref_ID=401802&paged=1

An unoptimized URL can be off-putting to users - it looks as if it could lead anywhere. Neither does it help with SEO because it has no keywords and doesn't describe the content.

You may find your content publishing system creates optimized URLs out-of-the-box, otherwise you'll need to change it. WordPress, for example, uses this type of permalink format for web pages and posts by default:

http://www.yoursite.com/?p=123

To change it, go to *Settings > Permalinks*, select *Post name* and click *Save changes*. This will give your posts and pages SEO-friendly URLs like the first example above.

Although it's best to set your permalinks to this format when you start publishing, if you need to make a change later WordPress automatically redirects old URLs to the new ones - meaning no loss of visitors or search engine traffic.

Forcing *www*.yoursite.com

Sometimes websites are accessible with both *www*.yoursite.com and just *yoursite.com*. In other words, there are two URLs leading to the same homepage - and every other page on the site. That could cause what's called a *duplicate content penalty* in search engines because it's a technique used by spammers to rank multiple times with the same pages.

To test whether you have this problem, type your domain name in a browser address bar and hit Enter. Do this once using *www.* before your domain and once without. Watch the browser address bar carefully both times.

No matter which version is used, you should be redirected to the same URL.

If not - and your homepage is visible both with and without the *www* prefix - you'll need to fix the problem. Look in your web hosting control panel for an option that allows you to specify that only the *www* version is used. If you can't find an option to do that, contact your hosting support.

If you're using an up-to-date version of WordPress, this feature is built-in so there's no need for you to do anything.

Keep your post slugs short

The slug is the last part of the post URL, formed by the title in lowercase with spaces converted to dashes. For example, if you write a post called *12 Ways to Enjoy the Amazingly Romantic Nightlife of Paris*, your post slug would be:

12-ways-to-enjoy-the-amazingly-romantic-nightlife-of-paris

Unfortunately, studies have also shown that users are less likely to click web addresses that are overly long with lots of dashes because they think of them as "spammy". Long slugs also tend to dilute the effectiveness of the keywords they contain.

Shorter post slugs are also more user-friendly because they're easier to read and less likely to get split into multiple lines when shared by email, which sometimes means the link no longer works.

If you're using WordPress, you can edit the post slug by clicking the edit button under the *Post Title* box.

WordPress Video Tutorial - How to Use Widgets

Permalink: http://www.geniusstartup.com/ wordpress-widgets / OK

In our example, the original *12 ways-to-enjoy-the-amazingly-romantic-nightlife-of-paris* could be shortened to *nightlife-of-paris* or even just *paris-nightlife*.

This kind of quick edit before you publish will give your posts short, keyword-rich URLs that work better for both users and SEO.

Setting up an XML Sitemap

A sitemap is a complete list of all the pages on your website that helps search engines easily find and index all of your site content.

Submitting an updated sitemap to Google when you publish new content means it gets added to Google faster.

Note: the type of sitemap referred to here is an XML file designed to be read by search engines, rather than a special page some sites have to help human visitors find their way around.

If you're using WordPress, setting up a sitemap is a two-step process.

1. Install the *Google Sitemap Generator* plugin which creates your sitemap and automatically updates it when you publish new content:

http://wordpress.org/extend/plugins/google-sitemap-generator/

2. Let Google know where your sitemap is by adding the sitemap URL to your site profile in *Google Webmaster Tools* under *Optimization > Sitemaps*.

Once you've done both those things, you won't need to do anything further - the plugin will send a notification to Google (as well as Yahoo! and Bing) every time you publish something new.

If you're publishing a substantial amount of video content, it's worth setting up a specific video sitemap:

http://wordpress.org/plugins/xml-sitemaps-for-videos/

If you're not using WordPress and need another way to generate a sitemap, take a look at this site which can create one from a URL:

http://www.xml-sitemaps.com/

Meta Tags

In SEO, there are three meta tags for web pages: title, description and keywords.

The title meta tag is formed from your page title, so in most cases it's automatically generated.

The keywords tag was designed to provide a list of keywords related to content. Because of abuse by spammers it's no longer used by Google or any other major search engine, so there's no need to use it.

The meta description tag lets you provide a description search engines can use when listing the page. While they have no impact on your rankings, a well written meta description will increase the number of people who click through to your site. Below is an example of good meta description.

26 Tips for Writing Great Blog Posts | Social Media Examiner
www.socialmediaexaminer.com/26-**tips**-for-**writing**-great-**blog**-posts/ ▾
Jan 23, 2012 - Want to get the most out of your business **blogging**? Follow thes **tips** to create optimal **blog** posts every time you sit down to write.

The most effective descriptions:

- Are around 160 characters long
- Are unique to the page
- Accurately convey what the page is about
- Make the user want to click the link

It's important to remember that search engines may not always use your description in their results. Google, in particular, often pieces together its own summary based on the parts of the page that are most relevant to a search query. Below in an example of an automatically generated description.

Writing a Good Blog - For Dummies
www.dummies.com/how-to/content/**writing**-a-good-**blog**.html ▾
Blogs , or Web logs, are online journals that are updated frequently. ... **Blogs** are for their casual **writing** and unpredictable subject material, but the best .... With recipes, entertaining & decorating **tips**, and more — we've got you covered!

As you can see, sometimes the description is a little garbled. Most content publishing systems give you the option to add a description to your pages. In WordPress you can use this plugin to set the meta description:

http://wordpress.org/plugins/wordpress-meta-description/

If you need to add it manually, the tag should be placed in the *<head>* part of your page in this format:

```
<meta name="description" content="Awesome
Description Here">
```

<u>Note</u>: if you need to use quote marks in your description, make sure you only use single quotes - double quotes cause Google to cut the summary at that point. They may also causes the page to display incorrectly in the browser.

STEP 4
Social Media Marketing

Using Social Sharing Buttons

Social signals - how many times a piece of content is shared, tweeted and liked - have become a crucial part of the way search engines decide which content is the most useful and should be ranked higher.

In other words, if two pieces of content are equal in terms of content quality, length and keyword usage, the one generating the greatest amount of social network activity will be ranked higher.

To help your content attract as many social signals as possible, make sure you've got sharing buttons for the major networks close to your content. People are lazy, and if they have to hunt for ways to share the content they may not bother. Effective locations to place buttons include just above or below the content.

A floating bar that remains in a fixed position as the reader scrolls down the page (so that the buttons are always in view) also works well with many site designs. This kind of effect can easily be achieved using one of the services / plugins listed below, even if you're not much of a coder.

Some services like *ShareThis* also allow you to track how often readers share your posts, which helps you focus on writing on the kind of content most appreciated by your audience.

http://sharethis.com/

http://wordpress.org/extend/plugins/sharebar/

http://wordpress.org/extend/plugins/sexybookmarks/

Don't forget to draw attention to your social buttons every once in a while. Simply asking readers who enjoyed a post to share it can have a dramatic effect on the number who do.

It's always worth trying different size buttons and layout positions - what works on another site might not work so well for you.

Experimenting while keeping an eye on the Social report of Google Analytics, will help you find the best combination for you and your audience.

One of the best things about using social buttons is that once in place, they require no further work on your part. But over time, the build-up of Likes, tweets and +1s will have a major impact on your SEO.

Even if you're not active on Facebook, Google+ or Twitter, have social sharing buttons for those networks on each piece of content you produce. If your content uses a lot of images, you'll also want buttons for Pinterest, Tumblr and other image-led networks.

If your content is useful to small businesses, freelancers or a specific profession, you'll probably get good traction from a LinkedIn button too.

Social Media Marketing for SEO

Not so long ago, SEO and social media marketing were different things. The idea was that SEO attracted visitors and social media marketing kept them coming back.

These days the two are intertwined. Google and other search engines increasingly use positive social signals as a major factor in ranking.

The trouble with social media is that it can quickly become a huge time-suck. That's partly because it's easy to get side-tracked into looking at hilariously grumpy cats or dream travel destinations, and partly because if you follow the standard advice you feel you need to be everywhere all at once.

Not only will that overwhelm you, it's physically impossible to do well and above all it isn't necessary. Instead, pick one or two networks you like and concentrate on those. You'll get a lot more mileage from focusing your efforts on a network you like rather than feel you have to be active on all of them.

Social media from an SEO point-of-view

At the time of writing, Google lists over 3.1 billion pages for the phrase "social media", 14 billion for "twitter" and 19 billion for "facebook". But almost all of that content is about building an audience for your Facebook page or Twitter account. Much less of it covers getting visitors from the social networks to your website.

Here's a no-fluff guide to doing just that - tips you should be following for each social network you're on.

Use a custom profile picture

Never use the default icon. It's unfriendly and makes your account look like a fake or spam account.

Even if you're representing a company, it's better to use a headshot than a logo or icon as your profile picture - people like to see who they're dealing with.

Add your web address to your profile

In most cases you'll want to link to your homepage, but if there's room you may also want to link directly to key pages on your site. Be sure to check the links work - it's too important a thing to risk a typo sneaking in.

Make users want to visit your site

What's written in your bio or about text is important. Make it short, snappy and give at least one reason why someone should visit your website - it may not be as obvious as you think to someone who's never heard of you.

Don't be tempted to buy followers or fans to make the numbers "look good"

You'll get no interaction – visits, revenue or otherwise – from these accounts. More importantly, Facebook and Twitter in particular, are clamping down on this kind of spam account.

Don't just post about yourself

Only sending updates about your latest blog post or "exciting" company news is a turn-off to users. Try to share links from others and join in conversations where you can. Once you've built an attentive, loyal audience you'll find that when you do post your own links you'll get more clicks.

Check regularly for comments

It looks bad if you're asked questions which are left unanswered.

Be pleasant, courteous and helpful at all times

Even if the other person seems unbelievably awful or awkward, you need to keep friendly and professional. Remember, your response could be online for a long time.

Double-check before posting

As well as checking spelling and grammar, look for hidden meanings. Without accompanying body language or facial cues, you might accidentally post something that could be read with (or without) a layer of sarcasm or irony that wasn't (or was) intended.

Be interesting

Before you post anything, ask why would my followers want to know this? If you can't think of a reason, drop it or change it.

Don't be afraid to repost your best content

Not everyone checks their Facebook, Twitter or Google+ accounts all day every day, so re-share your most popular posts. Older readers may have missed them and newer readers won't have seen them before. Obviously, you don't want overdo it but there's no harm in keeping your "greatest hits" visible.

Above all, remember that for SEO purposes, the idea is not to be popular on Facebook but to appear popular on Facebook. It's a subtle distinction that will improve your SEO efforts while saving you hours of work.

In other words, remember that from an SEO and traffic building perspective, the idea is not so much to build up Facebook's pages as to provide a springboard for visiting your site.

Specific Network Advice:
Facebook, Google+, Twitter and Pinterest

Google+ is the most important social network for website owners. Not only has it grown to become the second largest social network, sitting between Facebook (#1), and Twitter (#3), but because it's owned by Google it can give you tremendous SEO benefits.

It's not that Facebook, Twitter and other networks aren't important, it's just that Google+ is directly connected to Google, the most important search engine by far.

Because Google+ is smaller than Facebook, you'll probably find the number of *+1s* you get is lower than the number of Likes you get. But don't let that fool you. My experience has been that you get a lot more SEO mileage out of *+1s* than Facebook likes.

Here are some key ways to generate traffic from each of the main social networks.

Facebook

Post updates with pictures
Studies show that updates with pictures – especially featuring animals, babies and other cute things – get clicked on more than updates with no pictures.

Investigate using Facebook Apps
Many apps are free and they'll help you promote your content and links back to your site in more interesting ways that just a simple text update.

Expert advice
There are many Facebook "experts" but the "Queen of Facebook" (116,000+ Likes and counting) is Marie Smith. Find her (of course!) on Facebook: *https://www.facebook.com/marismith*

Twitter

Repeat your tweets

Twitter is fast-moving. When a tweet is more than an hour or two old, it's pretty much off the radar and not likely to get you much more traffic.

Given that, there's no harm in repeating tweets at different times of the day, to catch followers with different working times. One of the easiest ways to do that is with Hoot Suite which lets you queue, schedule and repeat your tweets as you like.

Connect your Twitter account to your Facebook profile

Once connected, tweets and links you publish will also appear on your Facebook page. To activate, go to *Settings > Profile* in Twitter.

Expert advice

One of the best online guides to Twitter marketing comes from Kiss Metrics: *http://blog.kissmetrics.com/2013-twitter-marketing-guide/*

Google+

Two core concepts of Google+, Circles and the +1 Button have a direct effect on your Google search results ranking.

Show the +1 button prominently on your site

The more people +1 your content the higher it will be shown in relevant Google search results.

Get more people in your Circles

Content created by people that are in a searcher's Circles is shown higher in Google search results. That means the more Circles you're in, the better.

Post Google+ updates to your new content

Google+ updates often appear in search results and links posted in Google+ updates tend to appear on Google very quickly.

Expert advice

Easily the most comprehensive guide to Google+ is this hugely informative epic from Martin Shervington: *http://www.martinshervington.com/what-is-google-plus/*

Pinterest

Especially if your website has a strong visual aspect to it, Pinterest can be a major traffic generator.

Make it easy to Pin your images

Use the Pin It button to make it easier to share your images. This button also makes sure the correct image attribution link is generated, so you'll always get a link back to your site.

Comment on other people's pins and repins

Check to see who's pinning your images by going to *http://pinterest.com/source/yoursite.com/* (replacing yoursite.com with your own website) and thank them for sharing your content and add a link to another, related page on your site.

Expert advice

Take a look at this extensive guide from content marketing specialists Hubspot:

http://blog.hubspot.com/blog/tabid/6307/bid/31147/The-Ultimate-Guide-to-Mastering-Pinterest-for-Marketing.aspx

Niche Social Networking Sites

Like forums, niche social networking sites are a great place to find a highly engaged audience interested in the subjects your site covers.

By becoming an active member of a community you'll also find opportunities to network with other bloggers as well as an endless source of ideas for blog post ideas. The key thing is not to treat your time there as a one-way marketing announcement. Get involved, share links to other resources and only include your own links every once in a while.

All this takes time, but a relevant link on a popular niche network can send you traffic - and improve your SEO - for a long time to come.

Here are some of largest networks in the bigger niches.

Arts & Artists

Artists2Artists
http://www.artists2artists.net/

ArtRise
http://www.artrise.com/

Artpromotivate
http://www.artpromotivate.com/

Behance
http://www.behance.net/

Paintings I Love
http://www.paintingsilove.com/

Books & Reading

Library Thing
https://www.librarything.com/

Good Reads
http://www.goodreads.com/

Paperback Swap
http://www.paperbackswap.com/

Revish
http://www.revish.com/

Shelfari
http://www.shelfari.com/

Business & Entrepreneurship

Biznik
http://biznik.com/

Eurocircle
http://www.eurocircle.com/

eWomen Network
http://new.ewomennetwork.com/

Lawyrs.net
http://www.lawyrs.net/

Project Eve
http://www.projecteve.com/

Ryze.com
http://www.ryze.com/

Spoke.com
http://www.spoke.com/

StartupNation
http://www.startupnation.com/

Xing
http://www.xing.com/

Cars & Bikes

BikerOrNot
http://www.bikerornot.com/

Edmunds Automotive Forums
http://forums.edmunds.com/

MadWhips
http://www.madwhips.com/

Motortopia
http://www.motortopia.com/

The AutoLog
http://www.theautolog.com/

Velospace
http://velospace.org/node

Hobbies

Burda Style (sewing)
http://www.burdastyle.com/

Curbly (DIY)
http://www.curbly.com/

Knit Picks
http://www.knitpicks.com/

Instructables
http://www.instructables.com/

Raverly (knitting)
https://www.ravelry.com/

Environmental, Social Good & Sustainability

Care2
http://www.care2.com/

Make Me Sustainable
http://www.makemesustainable.com/

Food, Cooking and Wine

Adegga
http://www.adegga.com/

AllRecipes.com
http://allrecipes.com/

Bake Space
http://www.bakespace.com/

Big Oven
http://www.bigoven.com/

Bottle Notes
http://www.bottlenotes.com/

Family Oven
http://www.familyoven.com/

Group Recipes

http://www.grouprecipes.com/

Must Love Wine
http://www.mustlovewine.com/

Open Source Food
http://www.opensourcefood.com/

Snooth
http://www.snooth.com/

Winelog
http://www.winelog.net/

Wine Societies
http://www.winesocieties.com/

Games

Game Spot
http://www.gamespot.com/

Kaneva
http://www.kaneva.com/

Second Life
http://secondlife.com/

Health & Medical

Baby Center Community
http://community.babycenter.com/

Daily Strength
http://www.dailystrength.org/

Live Strong
http://www.livestrong.com/

My Cancer Place
http://mycancerplace.com/

One Health
http://www.onehealth.com/

Patients Like Me
http://www.patientslikeme.com/

Peertrainer
http://www.peertrainer.com/

RareShare (rare medical conditions)
http://www.rareshare.org/

Tudiabetes
http://www.tudiabetes.org/

Music & Cinema

Film Affinity
http://www.filmaffinity.com/

Hip-Hop.net
http://www.hip-hop.net/

Jaman
https://jaman.com/

Jamendo
http://www.jamendo.com/

Last.fm
http://www.last.fm/

Singin.com
http://www.singin.com/

Pets

Catster
http://www.catster.com/

Dogster
http://www.dogster.com/

Petster
http://petster.com/

Photography

500px
http://500px.com/

Fotolog
http://www.fotolog.com/

MyShutterSpace
http://www.myshutterspace.com/

Picture Social
http://www.picturesocial.com/

Productivity & Self-improvement

43 Things
http://www.43things.com/

Tools for Life
http://toolstolife.com/

Shopping

DealDigg
http://www.dealigg.com/

Etsy
https://www.etsy.com/

Judy's Book
http://www.judysbook.com/

thisnext.com
http://www.thisnext.com/

Sports

ActionProfiles
http://actionprofiles.com/

Athlinks.com
https://www.athlinks.com/

FanNation
http://www.fannation.com/

Golf Link
http://www.golflink.com/

Sportsvite
http://sportsvite.com/

Takkle
http://www.takkle.com/

Travel

BootsnAll
http://www.bootsnall.com/

WAYN
http://www.wayn.com/

Tango Diva
http://www.tangodiva.com/

TravBuddy
http://www.travbuddy.com/

Trip Advisor
https://www.tripadvisor.com/

Where Are You?
http://www.whereareyou.net/

Women's Interests

BlogHer
http://www.blogher.com/

Cafe Mom
http://www.cafemom.com/

Chick Advisor
http://www.chickadvisor.com/

Circle of Moms
http://www.circleofmoms.com/

Mommy Tracked
http://www.mommytracked.com/

Raising Them
http://www.raisingthem.com/

Work It Mom
http://www.workitmom.com/

Writers & Writing

Author Marketing Forum
http://authormarketingclub.com/

Book-in-a-week.com
http://www.book-in-a-week.com/

Kboards
http://www.kboards.com/

Trigger Street Labs
http://labs.triggerstreet.com/

Writer's Cafe
http://www.writerscafe.org/

Writers Network
http://www.writers-network.com/

Using Triberr to Double Your Traffic

Triberr is a kind of a cross between a social network for bloggers and a content syndication platform. You set your blog to update Triberr automatically when you post new content, and then join "tribes" of other bloggers who write on similar topics.

In the Tribal Stream you'll see the latest posts from the tribes you've joined and be able to share them easily with your followers on Facebook, Twitter, Google+ or LinkedIn - and while you're sharing someone's post, someone else is sharing one of your posts.

In other words, your posts get shared through the social networks of other bloggers as well as your own. It's an extremely powerful platform. Within a few days of joining Triberr, spending only around 30 minutes a day on the site, I'd doubled my traffic.

How Triberr works

Suppose you have 1,000 Twitter followers. That means when you tweet a link to your latest blog post the potential reach is 1,000 people. Now suppose you're in a single tribe that has 10 members and each member has 1,000 followers. If only half your tribemates share your latest post with their followers, the potential reach of the post is now:

1,000 followers
x 5

_____

= 5,000 people

Don't forget, that's just Twitter. Triberr also lets your Tribemates share your content via Facebook, Google+, StumbleUpon and LinkedIn.

In reality, the average number of Twitter followers for the other bloggers in my Tribes is a lot more than 1,000. Currently it's 22,226. You can also be a member of more than one Tribe and most tribes have many more than 10 members.

That's a lot of big numbers that multiply to get you more traffic.

Currently I have 243 tribemates in 15 tribes, giving me a total reach of 5,330,738. The traffic gain as a result of 30 minutes a day sharing new posts via Triberr is amazing. It's easily one of my biggest sources of traffic.

If you're not using Triberr, I highly recommend you investigate this amazing, free platform: *http://triberr.com*

STEP 5
Build Links

PageRank and Link Building

A core concept used by Google since its launch is PageRank. Simply put, the PageRank algorithm says the more links a page has from other pages on the web the higher it should rank.

In other words, each link you get counts as a vote for your page.

On top of that, the more links that pages linking to you have themselves, the more weight that "vote" is worth. That means your link building strategy should be to get as many links as possible from the most authoritative sites.

Remember that PageRank is just one part of the whole Google algorithm. It's important, but building links to improve PageRank on its own won't catapult you to page one of Google. SEO success needs engaging content and social sharing as well.

Natural link-building

In the past, standard SEO advice was to get as many links as possible to your site - regardless of the source - and use the same anchor text each time. These days, doing that will get you knocked out of Google in no time.

Instead, your goal should be to slowly build a profile of good quality, natural, relevant links. A link is considered to have those qualities if it:

- Enhances the content where it appears

- Hasn't been put there just to improve search
  rankings

Before looking at the best places to get links, a word about where not to get links.

Avoid "bad neighborhoods". These are sites Google associates with spamming - used only to get free links without publishing meaningful, original content. These include:

- Article directories

- Reciprocal link directories (either free or paid, where site owners are required to link back to the directory)

- Any link built by automated software or submission process

A few years ago, all of these techniques were standard SEO advice - which is why you still see them mentioned in out-of-date blog posts - but they should now all be avoided.

Paid links are another no-no, whether another site linking to yours, or on your site linking to another site (except for banner ads and ad networks like AdSense).

Finding sites to get links from

The chances are you already know the major sites in your specific niche through your interest in the subject and your social network connections. But a few targeted Google searches will often uncover new sites to get links from.

As well as searching for your main keywords, try related keywords. For example, if your main phrase is Italian cooking, spin-off phrases include:

pasta
prosciutto
Italian wine
Italian restaurants
Rome

While not all those phrases are directly related to Italian cooking, you can see how visitors to a site about Rome would still be interested in reading about Italian cooking.

For each new site you find, make a quick assessment. Authority sites tend to have been publishing for a while and have a lots of social shares and followers.

Check for other signs of credibility. Steer clear of sites that have lots of spam comments, have more ads than content, or seem untrustworthy or spammy in some way.

Once you've established it's a good quality site, read through the most recent posts to find content that would benefit from linking to one of your posts. This could be where you take the opposite opinion, where you add further info not covered in the original post, or (in the case of a resources list) where you feel your site would be a valuable addition to the list.

Suggest your link either through the post comments or by email. In many ways, email is the better option. People don't always check their comments regularly but they're always on top of their emails.

You'll get the best response with an email that's quick and to the point. Just briefly explain what your post is about and why the site owner might want to link to it. Of course, it doesn't do any harm if you can show them a post where you have linked to one of their posts. It's amazing how often you'll get a positive response, provided you:

- Keep the email to a few lines maximum

- Take the time to find out the site owners name and use it

- Make a sensible suggestion that helps them out

Before emailing, read enough of their site to get a good idea of what kind of things they publish. Use that knowledge to suggest areas where your content can fill in the gaps on their site.

"Loved your post on the '5 Best Free Family Day Trips in London', but have you heard about...."

Make sure you follow the site via social media and sign up for their mailing list so you can spot future opportunities.

Finding Target Sites With Linking Tools

One of the most time-consuming parts about link-building is actually finding places that will give you links. But with a little detective work you can get a list of sites linking to your competitors, which you can use as a shortcut to get your own. After all, if your competitor can get links from them, you should be able to as well.

You may have heard it's possible to find which sites link to another by using a Google search query like link:www.yoursite.com. Unfortunately, it's not the most reliable method - even Google admits this command has never listed all sites, just a "small subset". For more accurate results, use one of the free tools below. They'll help you discover blogs, resource lists and directories that link to other sites in your niche.

As a bonus, many of these tools also list the authority of the domain, meaning you can target sites that will give you the most SEO value first.

http://www.ahrefs.com

http://www.blekko.com
This search engine lets you view SEO data on any domain, but it's a little more complicated than others on this list. First, you need to search for the domain, then click the link called SEO under the first search result.

http://www.linkdiagnosis.com

http://www.opensiteexplorer.org

http://www.seoattack.org

Tips for building links

Get links from as many domains as possible
In almost every niche, high-ranking sites have a greater number of domains linking to them than lower-ranking sites.

Get links from long-established sites

Sites that have been active for several years or more tend to have more "voting" clout than newer domains.

Use a variety of link types

A high number of links from a single type of source - like forums or blog comments, for example - may raise a spam flag. Keep an eye on the type of links you're getting in Google Webmaster Tools and try to even things out if your profile seems to be skewing towards a particular type of link.

Vary your anchor text

Hundreds of links that all use identical linking text is a sure-fire way to trigger the spam part of search algorithms. Use a variety of words and phrases in links back to your site and make sure they're not all highly-optimized keyword phrases. The aim is to be natural.

Web Directories

Web directories are as old as the web itself. Before the rise of Google and other search engines, they were the only way to find new sites on the internet.

These days, directory links are unlikely to generate a torrent of traffic but they're a good way to build external links to your site. Additionally, links from specialized directories in your niche will bring in a steady stream of targeted visitors and help reinforce your site's topic with Google.

For this reason, I've found it's better to get five or six listings on general directories and then concentrate on specialist directories.

General Web Directories

There are hundreds - probably thousands - of blog directories out there. Some are good, some are bad and some are only there to charge site owners a listing fee.

Below is a list of the 15 biggest blog directories that have a free submission process.

http://www.blogarama.com
http://www.blogcatalog.com
http://www.blog-directory.org
http://www.blogexplosion.com
http://www.bloggingfusion.com
http://www.bloglisting.net
http://www.blogs.com
http://www.blogville.us
http://www.globeofblogs.com
http://www.icerocket.com
http://www.ontoplist.com
http://www.paperblog.com
http://www.spillbean.com

http://www.technorati.com
http://www.topofblogs.com

Finding Directory Links in Your Niche

Use these types of searches to track down sites that can give you links:

your topic links
your topic resources
your topic websites
your topic directory

Once you've found a target site, look for a link submission form. If you can't find one, send a friendly note via the contact form or site email address.

The Free Web Directories List categorizes directories by region and specialist topic. It's definitely worth exploring if you have a niche interest website or one that relates to a specific geographical region: *http://www.web-directories.ws*

Web Design Directories

Another source of links are the many design showcase sites. If you have a stunning custom design, or a template design customized in a unique or beautiful way it's worth taking a few minutes to submit your site.

http://www.bestwebgallery.com
http://www.cssdesignawards.com
http://www.divinecss.com
http://www.makebetterwebsites.com
http://www.moluv.com
http://www.siteinspire.net
http://www.styleboost.com
http://www.unmatchedstyle.com
http://www.webcreme.com
http://www.welovewp.com
(specializes in WordPress sites)

Curated Content: Getting Featured on Link Roundups & More

Sometimes called curation blogging, content curation means posting collections of useful links, videos, podcasts, infographics, and resources on a specific theme, along with a little informed commentary.

Done well, this type of in-depth, comprehensive post is popular with visitors and Google (which loves content that links to authoritative sources).

A good example of this type of post are link round-ups like Kristi Hines' *Fetching Friday*. Every week Kristi features stories related to writing, marketing, productivity and personal development for bloggers. Check out Fetching Friday at: http://kikolani.com/category/fetching-friday

Finding link round-ups

It can be a bit tricky to find out who's publishing link round-ups because not everyone uses that name. That said, here are some searches you can try that turn up results in most niches:

link roundup [your topic]
daily link roundup [your topic]
weekly link roundup [your topic]
daily links [your topic]
weekly link [your topic]

If that doesn't reveal anything worthwhile, take a look at other blogs and sites in your niche - there's usually someone, somewhere publishing this kind of post.

A close relation of the link roundup are link parties (also called blog hops). These are non-curated links lists, where the host blog lets other bloggers post links on a particular theme. The key to getting traffic from blog hops is to post early, so you're near the top of the list, and to use an attention-grabbing headline.

Link parties are more popular in some niches than others, notably subjects like crafts, recipes, fitness, organizing, weddings, and parenting.

Writing your own weekly link roundup post

Because Google likes sites that link out to good quality content, publishing your own curated content can be a very smart move.

The trick is only to include the most valuable and useful links on a specific theme.

Make sure you tell readers why you recommend a link and provide a mix of links from both big and not so big blogs so that even the biggest media junkies will find something new.

Send the link to everyone featured in your post - the chances are high that they will link back to you or share the link with their followers.

Regular curated content can be quite time-consuming to put together - but not as time-consuming as writing a new blog post from scratch - and there are some good tools out there that can really speed up the process - my current favorite is CurationSoft (*http://curationsoft.com*).

Blog Carnivals

Blog carnivals are an ongoing series of posts that link to articles on a particular theme. They're a sort of cross between curated content and a mini-magazine. Depending on the carnival organizer, posts are either published on the same blog each week or on different blogs in turn. Submissions are usually coordinated through a central point.

Taking part in a popular blog carnival will bring a steady stream of visitors from blogs on a similar theme to yours, which means you're likely to pick up new regular readers.

Like guest posting, being part of a carnival brings your work to the attention of a lot of readers quickly, but unlike guest posting you're writing for your own site, not someone else's.

All those new inbound links to your site are good for SEO too.

Submitting to blog carnivals is as easy as finding one that fits the theme of your site and suggesting material to the organizer.

To find blog carnivals, try searching for *[your subject] blog carnival.* You'll also find an extensive directory of carnivals categorized by topic at *http://blogcarnival.com.*

STEP 6
Speed Up Your Site

Why Site Loading Time Matters

Successful sites load fast. Even a small delay can have an impact on visitor numbers and conversions.

When Firefox shaved just 2.2 seconds from the download time of its browser, conversions increased by a whopping 15.4%.

Site loading speed has been important for good search engine rankings for a number of years. Google recognizes that even if a site looks promising in search results, users will be disappointed if they have to hit the back button because the site is taking too long to load.

How long is too long?

Different surveys give different figures, but most experts agree there's a noticeable loss of traffic if the delay is more than three seconds. That doesn't mean the entire page should load in three seconds, but the basic content and layout should load in that time allowing visitors to start using the page as quickly as possible.

That means if your site is taking longer than 5-6 seconds to load there's room for improvement. If it takes 10 seconds or longer the delayed loading time is almost certainly dragging your site down in search results.

Aim to have the basic content and design to load in 2-3 seconds, with the remaining images and dynamic content loading over the following few seconds.

Checking your loading time

It's a good idea to check loading time before optimizing your site, as well as after each step in this section to see the improvement you're making. There are quite a few places to do this but one of the easiest to use is the *Full Page Test* tool at Pingdom.com.

Type in your domain name and the test will give an overall performance grade and tell you how long each element takes to load. This lets you see where the biggest bottlenecks are so you optimize those first. Bookmarking the report page will give you an archived benchmark report to refer to as you optimize.

For accurate results, run checks at the same time of day to make sure loading times aren't affected by periods when the web in general is busier or slower. Spacing tests at least 24 hours apart is a good idea to be sure browser and other web caches have cleared between tests.

Go on a Widget and Plugin Diet

Too many widgets and plugins can really slow your site down, so both need to be used sparingly.

Widgets are often one of the biggest bandwidth hogs on a site, so reducing the number used will make a quick and dramatic improvement to site loading times.

Some widgets are useful, but on many sites the sidebar ends up as a collection of slow loading ornaments that contribute nothing to the user experience. All those Tweet, Facebook and other "news" panels might look pretty but because widgets pull in data from external sites they're almost always the slowest loading elements on a page.

Having too many widgets also tends to make a site look like an amateur personal blog.

Be ruthless. Drop anything that's not essential. When was the last time you visited a site and were glad you could see a stream of personal Flickr photos or where the last ten visitors came from?

Likewise, have a serious think about replacing that slow-loading Twitter widget with the standard icon. It'll load instantly and when you think about it, readers don't really need to see your latest tweets on every page of your site.

Slim down your sidebar and watch your site performance rocket.

If you're using WordPress, remember that too many plugins will slow down your site performance by loading additional files and running extra database queries. The more plugins you have installed, the more the problem is multiplied.

As with widgets, time spent weeding out plugins that aren't essential will really pay off.

Head over to the *Plugins* page of your WordPress dashboard. Click the *Inactive* link at the top and you'll see plugins that are installed but aren't in use. Given they're inactive, chances are you don't need them.

Although inactive plugins don't contribute directly to site loading time, they do slow down the admin area as it checks regularly for plugin updates. Out-of-date plugins are also a common security hole used by hackers to gain access to sites, so it's a good idea to delete any you don't need.

Next, click the *Active* link on your plugins page.

Like widgets, it pays to be selective and keep only those that are useful. If you've been trying out different image slider plugins, for example, and have found one you like, deactivate and delete the others.

If you're confident with editing theme files, remember that some plugins can be replaced by adding a few lines of code (or less) to a template. For example, there are a number of plugins that add the Google Analytics tracking code, but a simple copy and paste of the code into the header.php file of your theme will load faster and mean you need one less plugin.

For every plugin you're using, consider whether the user experience would be diminished without it. If the answer is no, that's a plugin that can go.

Setting Up a Cache Plugin

If you're using WordPress, installing a cache plugin is another quick fix that can dramatically improve site performance.

Because WordPress stores content and data in a database, each page load needs a number of database queries to transfer that content and data to the web browser. The next time someone visits the page, the same set of queries are run all over again - even if the visit is just a few seconds later and the content hasn't changed.

A cache plugin creates static copies of your pages and sends those to browsers instead. Because static copies aren't generated by database queries, they load much faster. To stop pages becoming out-of-date, the cache plugin creates a new, updated copy at regular intervals.

There are a few cache plugins for WordPress, but the two I recommend are *WP Super Cache* and *Total Cache*. Both can be installed directly from the WordPress dashboard by going to Plugins > Add New and searching for them by name. You can also find out more about them here:

Total Cache
http://wordpress.org/extend/plugins/w3-total-cache/

WP Super Cache
http://wordpress.org/extend/plugins/wp-super-cache/

While *Total Cache* has many more features, it's more complicated to configure and I've found it can be tricky to get to work with some web hosting configurations. There's no doubt it's a great plugin, but, unless you're a technical whizz, my recommendation is to use *WP Super Cache* - it's just as good but easier to set up.

Configuring WP Super Cache

Once installed, the plugin will add an extra menu item under *Settings >*

WP Super Cache. Click that link and you'll be taken to the *Easy* configuration panel. This has one setting at the top, *Caching On.* Make sure that's selected, then click the *Update Status* button.

This is the minimum you need to do get the plugin running, but there are a couple of extra settings that will make the performance even better. Click on the *Advanced* tab. You'll see there are many more options on this page. Here's a list of the options I've found to work well. Make sure all the options on the list below are checked, leaving everything else unchecked.

Cache hits to this website for quick access
This should already be checked.

Use mod_rewrite to serve cache files

Compress pages so they're served more quickly to visitors

Don't cache pages for known users
Prevents logged in users seeing cached content, which means as an admin user you'll see changes instantly when updating your site.

Don't cache pages with GET parameters

Cache rebuild...

Extra homepage checks

You may need to adjust these settings a little, but I've found they work great for 95% of sites.

After you click *Update Status* to save your settings, you may see a message telling you to update your "Mod_Rewrite Rules". This can be done with a button further down the same page.

One last thing to do is set the *Cache Timeout* and *Scheduler.* Both of these are further down the *Advanced* tab, under the heading *Expiry Time & Garbage Collection.*

Cache Timeout sets how many seconds a page copy remains in the cache before being updated. A good setting for this is 3600 seconds (one hour).

Next, select *Scheduler* and set the value to 3600. This sets how often static pages no longer being used are cleared from the server.

These two settings will work well for most sites, but take a look at the settings suggested by the plugin on that page to see which is likely to work best for your site.

When you're done, click *Change Expiration* to save.

After making changes to the cache settings, check your website to make sure everything is running as it should be. Remember you'll need to be logged out - like a normal visitor - to see the cached version.

If you're not used to doing this kind of thing, all these settings may seem a bit daunting but in reality it's pretty straightforward. There's also a fantastically helpful support forum for *WP Super Cache* at:

http://wordpress.org/support/plugin/wp-super-cache

Minify HTML, CSS and Javascript files

Even the tidiest of web code has extra spaces and line breaks in it. Minifying code means to strip out all these extras in HTML, CSS, Javascript and other files.

It might not sound like something that could have much of an impact on file loading time, but minifying code can give a speed boost of anywhere between 10 and 30%.

If you're using the Total Cache plugin you'll find it has a minify feature that does a great job of compressing code. Otherwise, take a look this plugin:

http://wordpress.org/plugins/bwp-minify/

As with using a cache plugin, once you've activated minifying, it's a good idea to throughly check the output of your site to be sure everything is OK.

If you're not using WordPress, or don't want to compress code automatically, take a look at minifycode.com which lets you paste in or upload HTML, CSS and Javascript code and create a compressed version.

Making Images Load Faster

There's no doubt that good use of images can really help bring your site to life and get your message across - not too mention increase "shareability" on social networks - but be careful not to overdo it.

The key to optimizing images is to make sure each one is serving a useful purpose (do you really need that 1200 by 700 pixel header image?) and that the file size is as small as possible.

How to compress your image file size

If you're creating your own images, use the most amount of image compression you can before the quality starts to degrade. There's no visual difference between a JPEG image exported at 100% and one exported at 85% but the difference in file size is huge.

Even JPEGs exported at 80% are often fine for web use.

Likewise, use the best format for the type of image - photography looks best as a JPEG. Most other types of image look best - and have a smaller file size - when exported as a PNG.

WordPress users have the option of a plugin that automatically compresses each new image as you upload. It can also run through images you've already uploaded and compress those.

Take a look at the plugin here:
http://wordpress.org/extend/plugins/wp-smushit

If you need an online image optimizer, take at look at:
http://www.imageoptimizer.net

Use Reliable & Fast Web Hosting

The other techniques in this section won't be as effective as they should be if your web hosting is too slow and unable to deliver files quickly.

Speed is often a problem on cheap, unoptimized shared hosting because there are thousands of sites hosted on a single server. That means just a few busy or badly run sites can hog too much server power and slow response times for you and everyone else on the same server.

Free hosting services suffer the same problem but on a larger scale. Since no one is paying for the service, an even greater number of sites are crammed into the servers to keep costs down. That's not to mention that free hosting usually runs ads on your site and won't let you use your own domain name (a major disadvantage for SEO).

Recommended web hosts

Media Temple
http://www.mediatemple.net

Over the past 15 years I've used a number of hosting companies but since 2008 I've been with Media Temple exclusively. They are easily the best I've used. Service is great, there are few problems and when I do need support I can speak to someone friendly and knowledgeable by phone or web chat any time of the day or night.

While they offer dedicated and VPS hosting, I use the Grid Server plan (an optimized shared hosting that runs super fast) which costs $20 a month. That's more expensive than most shared hosting but much cheaper than dedicated hosting, which is what would normally be needed for the half a million monthly pageviews the sites on my account generate.

Give that I still have almost half of my bandwidth unused and there's a free Content Distribution Network (see the next chapter) thrown in, I think it's a great deal.

HostGator

http://www.hostgator.com

If you're on a budget, check out HostGator. Many of my clients and contacts host with HostGator and it's hard to find anyone with a bad word to say about them. With every plan you get unlimited disk space / bandwidth / email accounts, 99.9% uptime guarantee and a 45-day money back guarantee.

If you visit the HostGator link above, make sure you use the coupon code ***genius25off*** - it'll give you a bonus 25% off.

Using a Content Distrubution Network (CDN)

With standard web hosting, one copy of your site is located on a server in, say, Los Angeles. The further a user is from Los Angeles the slower the site will load because the files have to travel further over the internet.

The distances don't have to be that large to make a measurable difference - anything over several hundred miles will cause a noticeable delay, with users on a different continent to the server experiencing even greater delays.

With a Content Delivery Network, multiple copies of your site are hosted on a network of servers around the world. Typical locations might include Chicago, New York, Los Angeles, Miami, Seattle and Toronto in North America; Amsterdam, Frankfurt, London, Paris and Stockholm in Europe; Hong Kong, Singapore, Sydney and Tokyo in Asia / Australia.

Instead of all connections going through Los Angeles, users connect to their nearest network location. This gives a huge improvement in loading times.

Web giants like Amazon, Facebook and Google have used this type of technology for years, but recently a number of companies have made CDNs affordable for the rest of us.

With all the companies below, the system is more or less automatic. Once configured, the CDN automatically keeps the network servers updated. All you have to do is keep publishing as normal.

Amazon CloudFront
http://aws.amazon.com/cloudfront/
One of the biggest names in the business. Pricing is somewhat confusing and it doesn't offer a flat monthly rate, charging instead per GB transferred starting at $0.120 per GB.

CDN77

http://www.cdn77.com/
Popular but somewhat pricey option which starts at $49 per month.

MaxCDN

http://www.maxcdn.com/
Plans start from $9 a month, enjoys a good reputation.

Free Content Distribution Networks

There are two major CDNs that have a free option.

The first, *CoralCDN*, is an open source, 100% free option but having tested it on a couple of sites I recommend staying away from it. When comparing loading stats before and after using CoralCDN I found it actually slowed the sites down. Obviously, that's disastrous for SEO and I'm only mentioning it as a warning.

The second option, *CloudFlare*, is a mostly premium service ($20 a month) but customers of Media Temple can use it for free.

Once you're logged into your account center, the CloudFlare activation options are on the first page. You'll need to activate it for each domain you want to use it on. Other than that, there's no setup process.

Other well-known hosting companies that currently offer CloudFlare include:

1&1 Hosting
Bluehost
HostGator

More SEO Resources & Next Steps

Using Google Analytics

By measuring how many visits your site is getting, you can see how well your search engine optimization is working and see which SEO strategies get the best results.

Google Analytics is the industry standard for measuring website audiences. By adding a small snippet of Javascript code to your website, you'll have access to detailed statistics on just about every aspect of user interaction with your site.

At a glance, you'll be able to see things like:

- Which search engine, keywords and social networks send you the most traffic

- The most popular pages on your site

- How long visitors stay on your site and the sequence of pages visited

- Geographical breakdowns by county, state, and city

And that's just scratching the surface.

How to add Google Analytics to your site

The first step is to sign up for a free account: *http://www.google.com/analytics/*

Once you've signed up, click the *Admin* tab near the top of any page in Analytics. On the next page click the button that says + *New Property (web or app).*

Then complete the short form under the heading *Setting up your web property.* You'll need to fill in *Website Name, Web Site URL, Industry Category* and *Reporting Time Zone.*

Under *Web Site URL*, make sure you enter only the domain name with the www prefix. In other words, if your homepage is *http://www.yoursite.com/* then you should enter *www.yoursite.com* as the *Web Site URL*.

Set the *Reporting Time Zone* to your time zone and then click *Get Tracking ID*.

At this point, you've added your site to Google Analytics but you still need to add the tracking code to your site to generate visitor reports.

If you've just set up your website's property profile using the instructions above, you should have the snippet of Javascript which is your tracking code. If you ever need to find the tracking code again, just click on *Admin* at the top of any Analytics page, choose the website you want to track then click the *Tracking Info* tab.

Adding the tracking code to your site manually

If you're comfortable with editing your site source files, open the template that contains the *<head>* section and copy and paste your tracking code just above the closing *</head>* tag. Save and upload the file and you're done.

Adding the tracking code with a WordPress plugin

If you're using WordPress and don't want to edit your theme files directly, you can use a plugin to add the tracking code for you.

Here are two recommended plugins, both free from the official WordPress.org plugin directory.

The first, just called *Google Analytics*, is ideal if you want to get the tracking code running on your site without whistles and bells:

http://wordpress.org/extend/plugins/googleanalytics/

The second, *Google Analytics for WordPress*, includes support for advanced tracking features like counting clicks to external sites and file downloads (useful if you want to measure how many times a promotional ebook has been downloaded, for example).

It also adds website statistic reports to the WordPress dashboard. You'll still need to go to Google Analytics to access the full range of data, but the reports generated by the plugin are great for getting a quick overview of your stats.

Find out more about the plugin here:

http://wordpress.org/extend/plugins/google-analytics-for-wordpress/

If you're not used to installing plugins, the easiest way is to add them directly from your WordPress admin by choosing *Plugins > Add New* from the main menu and then searching for the name of the plugin.

If you prefer to add the tracking code manually, open the header.php file of your theme and paste your tracking code just above where you see the *</head>* tag, then upload the new version of the file to your site.

Remember that if you change your WordPress theme, you'll need to add the tracking code to the header.php file of your new theme.

If you're using another content management system you'll need to paste the tracking code in the header part of your templates. Check the online documentation or support for your platform to find out where to add the code.

Once you've added the tracking code to your site, don't forget to check it's working.

The easiest way to do that is visit your site a few times and then check that the Tracking Info tab in Google Analytics (Admin > Tracking Info) says "Receiving Data" under Status.

Don't worry if you don't see that message immediately. I've found new tracking codes can take up to a couple of hours to start showing data when first activated.

Now that your account is running and tracking visitors, let's take a crash course on the key statistics you should be keeping an eye on – and how to find them within the interface.

Audience Overview

Clicking *Audience > Overview* from the left menu displays a graph of day-by-day traffic over the last 30 days. This gives you a quick snapshot of monthly visits.

You'll see two statistics listed under the graph - *Visits* and *Unique Visitors*.

Visits
This is the total number of visits for your site as a whole.

Unique Visitors
The total number of completely different visitors to a site, not counting repeat visits by the same person in the same time period. If someone visits on Monday and returns on Friday, that's two visits but only one unique visitor.

As with all the reports in Google Analytics, there are a variety of filtering options you can apply to this report.

One of the easiest and most useful is to take a look at the big picture by changing the date option at the top right to cover the last year or six months. The resulting graph is an instant overview of whether you're increasing or decreasing visitors in the long-term. Although there will naturally be highs and lows in the graph, overall you should be able to see a steady upward trend.

If it is, you know your marketing and SEO efforts are paying off. Otherwise, review the steps in this book to see if there are areas that could be worked on more.

Digging into reports like *Search Engine Optimization* and *Social* – both under *Acquisition* – will tell you which sources are the reason for the increase or decrease in traffic.

You can also compare visitor numbers between two date ranges within the same report. To do that, click the date dropdown select near the top-right of the page, select *Compare to*, choose a date range, and then click the *Apply* button.

The report now shows the two time periods in one graph and gives you comparative figures underneath.

Content / Pageviews

Pageviews are the number of pages viewed on your site during a given time. You can get a detailed report by viewing Behaviour > Site Content. On that page you'll see a graph of pageviews per day, along with a list of the most visited pages.

Pageviews
A straightforward total of how many pages were viewed. Every time a visitors loads a page that's one pageview.

Unique pageviews
This number will almost always be less than Pageviews because it's the number of <u>individual</u> pages viewed by visitors. Each different page is counted only once, no matter how many times it was viewed in total.

For example, if a visitor arrives at your homepage, goes to the About page and then clicks back to the homepage that's three pageviews but only two <u>unique</u> pageviews.

Other key terms

Bounce Rate

When viewing both of the previous reports, you've probably noticed the term *bounce rate*.

This is the percentage of visitors who view only a single page before leaving, either because they close the browser or hit the back button.

The idea is to have a bounce rate as low as possible.

Realistically, if it's around 50-60% that's fine. Sites that have lots of visitors from search engines or social networks like Twitter and Facebook usually have a higher bounce rate. That's because visitors from those sources tend to visit the page they came for and leave immediately after.

If you find your bounce rate is 80% and above, there's definitely room for improvement. Try encouraging visitors to visit a second page on your site by including relevant links within your content, making the site navigation clearer or more inviting, or adding related posts to the bottom of your blog posts.

Avg. Visit Duration / Avg. Time on Page

Like bounce rate, these averages are a good indicator of how much visitors like your site. Although longer is better, anything between one and three minutes is about normal.

Remember to look at *Avg. Visit Duration* and *Avg. Time on Page* along with bounce rate. A high bounce rate with long visit times tells you that although people may only view one page, they tend to read it fully.

On the other hand, a high bounce rate coupled with short visit times should set off alarm bells - it shows visitors leave often and quickly. It's likely there's something fundamental about your site - bad design or a slow loading time, for example - that's driving people to the back button.

Social

The *Acquisition > Social* section of Google Analytics is quite in-depth and each subsection tells you something different about the profile of your site on social networks.

Overview
This is a quick view of how you're doing on the various networks. Google has quite a broad definition of "social network", so as well as Facebook, Twitter and the usual networks you may also see data on websites like Goodreads, Pocket and Quora.

Network Referrals
A list of networks on which your site is most popular. For more details, click on the network name and you'll see exactly which pages people are landing on from that network.

Data Hub Activity
In this report, a data hub is anywhere visitors can share, link to or otherwise spread the word about your site.

That could be a social network, Q&A sites like Quora or Stack Overflow, social bookmarking sites like Delicious or Diigo, distributed commenting platforms like Disqus or Livefyre, social news sites like Reddit, as well as sites and web apps that have a social or sharing component like Pocket or Meetup.

Under the *Activity Stream* - a graph that shows the level of activity per day, week or month - you'll find options to view detailed information that can be filtered by network / website. It's a great place to monitor your social media marketing efforts. If you're working on raising your Google+ profile, for example, you can use this *Data Hub Activity* report to quickly see if your efforts are paying off.

Note: At the time of writing, Facebook and Twitter aren't data hub partners - which means although you'll find them in the other reports, they're not included in the data hub report.

Landing Pages
Here you can find out which pages users most frequently arrive on from social sites. Clicking the listing for a page takes you to an in-depth report showing which social networks drove the most traffic to that page.

Trackbacks
Shows a list of the most recent websites and blogs that have linked to your content. It shows both the exact page where the link was posted as well as the page on your site they linked to - useful information for link-building.

Conversions
If you have an ecommerce site, this report will show how many of your visitors from social media convert to paying customers.

Plugins
Shows which social buttons are generating the most interaction, letting you see which buttons and positions work best with your design and content.

Visitor Flow
Here you can see the most common routes social media visitors take when landing on your site, filtered by social network. This is great for getting an overview of which network sends you the most traffic and to which page.

Depending on your content, you may find users from different social networks respond better to certain types of content. The *Visitor Flow* report helps you fine-tune your social media strategy so you can create content that's more likely to be shared on a particular network.

Search Engine Optimization

In this section you'll find the subsections *Queries*, *Landing Pages* and *Geographical Summary*.

Queries shows the keywords visitors used to find your site. Because the report also shows the average position for each keyword you rank for, it's one of the most accurate ways of tracking how well your SEO is going.

Bear in mind the data isn't real time and is delayed by up to two days.

<u>Note</u>: to get access to the full data for the *Search Engine Optimization* sections, you'll need a Google Webmaster Tools account and to have linked it with Google Analytics. See the next chapter for instructions on how to do this.

Keeping it in perspective

When viewing site statistics it's important not to get too fixated on this particular week or month. There's a normal ebb and flow with web traffic, beyond factors like holidays and seasons.

The key thing is to make sure that over longer periods like six months or a year, you can see a general upward trend. As long as you can see that, you're on the road to greater success.

Using Google Webmaster Tools

Wouldn't it be great if you could get inside the mind of Google and see what it actually thinks of your site?

One of the lesser-known Google apps, Google Webmaster Tools, lets you do exactly that. Not only does it provide keyword ranking data for every keyword your site ranks for, you'll get customized improvement recommendations and diagnostics tools.

Webmaster Tools is invaluable because it gives you a snapshot of how Google sees your site and what it knows about it.

It's also the most reliable way of checking your Google rankings. You might think you can do that easily by searching for your target phrases and seeing where your site appears in the results, but think again.

Because Google now heavily personalizes results based on location, browsing history, links shared by members of your social circle and other factors, the search results you see are different from those shown to other users. In particular, sites you've visited a number of times before or have shared via a social network, will tend to be shown higher in your personalized search results.

Using Webmaster Tools is a much more reliable way of checking your rankings because it shows the average ranking for individual pages.

To sign up for a free Webmaster Tools go to:
http://www.google.com/webmasters/

Once you have an account, you'll be prompted to add your first site. Part of this process involves verifying your site, a security feature that prevents someone getting access to data on sites they don't own.

There are a number of ways to verify a site. Most of these involve technical things like uploading a file via FTP or editing your DNS records, but the simplest option is to verify using your Google Analytics account. Because the tracking code is already installed on your site from the previous chapter, this option means there's nothing extra for you to do.

Just choose Google Analytics as your verification method (it may be hidden under the *Alternate Methods* tab on the verification page).

It can take a few days or longer for data on your site to start showing in Webmaster Tools, especially if your site is new. Bear in mind too, that because it's providing information based on the Google search index, there's a delay before new pages show up in the reports.

An optional, but highly recommended, step is linking Webmaster Tools to your Google Analytics account. It'll give you access to a lot of valuable, additional information in the *Search Engine Optimization* report of Google Analytics. To link the two together, click the *Admin* tab in Google Analytics and then click the *Property Settings* tab. At the bottom of the page you'll see an option to create a link under the heading Webmaster Tools Settings.

How to use Google Webmaster Tools

As with Google Analytics, there are a lot of reports in Webmaster Tools - many of which you won't normally need to look at - but check the *Search Traffic* reports regularly.

Under *Search Traffic* you'll find three subsections. Here's how each can help you.

Search Queries

Easily the most useful report in Webmaster Tools, this graph plots two key statistics over the last thirty days.

The blue line is the number of impressions (appearances) of your site in Google search results, the red line is the number of times a user clicked through and went to your site.

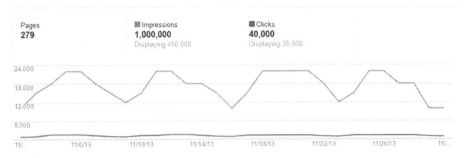

Under the graph there's a detailed text report of all the keywords Google has your site indexed under.

Links to Your Site

This report shows the three most important things you need to know about external links to your site.

Who links the most

A ranking table of sites that have the most links to your site. You can click on any domain name to see the specific page the site links to.

Clicking on any of the pages on that list will display the exact page on the external site that the link appears.

This link report, combined with the *Acquisition > All Referrals* report in Google Analytics, is an easy way to find sites like forums where you can get links easily and which send you traffic.

Your most linked content

These are the pages that have the most links pointing to them from around the web. Click through to the main table and you'll see both the number of links and the number of unique domains. This is another good place to see which content generates the most links back to your site, so that you can focus on similar subjects.

How your data is linked

This is a report of the most commonly used anchor text (the words that form a link) on other sites when they link to you. Anchor text is an important part of helping search engines understand what a post, page or website is about.

For example, if most of the external links to your site use the word "dog" in the linking text, Google will assume your site is about dogs.

It's important that anchor text is varied - links from many domains all using exactly the same anchor text might well trigger spam filters, for example. This report lets you check that things look natural.

Internal Links

An internal link is a link from one page on your site to another on your site. This report shows you which internal pages you're linking to the most. It's a good way to confirm the pages you most want visitors to visit - landing pages, mailing list opt-ins, or pages that perform well in AdSense - are being linked to frequently from within your site, making them easy to find for both search engines and visitors.

Other reports

Google is constantly updating the reports in Webmaster Tools, so it's worth exploring the other reports. In particular, keep an eye on *Search Appearance > HTML Improvements*, which alerts you to problems encountered when indexing the site.

One final tip, Webmaster Tools only shows data over the past thirty days. That means if you want to view records for longer, you need to download the data as .csv file for spreadsheet viewing. Most reports have a button allowing you to do that.

How to Recover From a Google Penalty

Search engine results are in a constant state of ebb and flow as rankings for individual pages and sites go up and down, outdated content fades and new pages are published. Because of that, you'll probably see an ebb and flow on your site rankings, especially if you're lower down in the results.

But sometimes you'll see a dramatic change of not just a place or two but ten or twenty places or even more. In severe cases a site may drop out of Google completely.

There are three reasons why a site falls in search engine results:

- Increased competition from other pages which rank better, pushing yours down

- Major changes have been made to your site or content that have had an adverse effect

- You've had a penalty applied to your site, causing your Google results to drop

Here's how to decide which applies to you and what to do about it.

Increased competition

If the decrease in rankings is relatively slight and happened gradually over the course of a month or more, you're probably just facing increased competition.

Sometimes it just happens that other sites sneak up from behind and leapfrog over you.

The only way forward is to outdo them. Try to create better content than anyone else, get more social shares and become more of an authority site than your competitors.

This is usually relatively easy to fix because it just means you need to do more of the things you should be doing anyway.

Site changes that have an adverse effect

If you can rule out the possibility of a Google penalty but the rankings slide seems to have started on a particular date, it could be there's been a change to your site that's had an adverse effect.

Do a thorough check of your site to make sure it's displaying correctly with no missing content or error messages. If you've recently added a feature or new site design it could be it's slowing the site speed down or causing other problems.

Check Google Webmaster Tools for problems encountered while Google tried to crawl your site. Pay particular attention to the *Crawl* and *Security Issues* sections.

The *Crawl* section lists errors encountered while trying to index your site, including URL and DNS errors. Take a look at the graph of URL errors - if you see a significant increase in errors on a particular date, especially if it's around the time of a slump in rankings - that's the likely cause.

A sustained period of DNS errors, which make it impossible to load your domain name, can cause a loss of rankings. If you see lots of these errors in the DNS report, check your nameservers are set correctly. This can be done through the control panel of your web hosting company or, if your domain name is registered somewhere else, in the admin panel of your domain registrar.

The *Security Issues* panel will show you if Google has detected malware or other security breaches on your site. If you find something listed here, it's important to sort out the problem as soon as possible. Google has an excellent series of walk-through tutorials to help you recover being hacked:
https://www.google.com/intl/en/webmasters/hacked/

You should also follow any instructions in the *Security Issues* panel.

Once you've fixed the problems, request re-inclusion in the index by going to the Google resource above and following the *Request a review* link.

The good news is Google is pretty quick at reviewing sites and recovered sites are usually restored to the index within a day or two.

Key signs of a Google penalty

If Google decides a site no longer adheres to its quality guidelines, they may apply a site-wide penalty pushing the results down for every page. The more infractions - and the greater the seriousness of the infractions - the bigger the penalty and the further the site will drop.

In the worst cases, a site will drop fifty or even hundreds of places, or be removed from the index completely.

The more of the following statements are true, the more likely it is you're suffering from a full or partial site-wide penalty.

- The drop is across the whole site, rather than just a few pages.

- The drop seems to have happened on a specific day. Check search engine blogs and forums for indications of an algorithm change on or around that date. Google sometimes announces changes, but not always.

- Your site no longer appears when you search for the domain name or another term unique to the site, like the site name.

If it looks like Google has applied a penalty to your site, you need to establish what caused it and correct the problem before submitting a re-inclusion request.

The reasons for a penalty can include any or all of these things:

Low-quality website

If your content is consistently very short and not original the Google algorithm is likely to consider the site low-quality. Examples include affiliate sites which duplicate product descriptions from Amazon, aggregation sites republishing content "as is" from elsewhere, and sites containing "spun" content (software generated rewordings of articles published elsewhere).

The solution is to publish longer, good quality, original content that readers will want to share.

Manipulative linking strategies

This includes paid links to another site on your site (except banner ads, AdSense, etc.), paid links to your site on someone else's, reciprocal link exchange programs involving large numbers of links from low-quality, paid listings directories, and the use of link farms - networks of sites designed to provide thousands of inbound links.

It's important to understand that a handful of reciprocal links is not going to do you any harm and neither are paid-for links in the form of legitimate advertising. The problem comes when it looks like there's an attempt to manipulate rankings with a mass of links that have been purchased or manipulated in some way.

The solution is simply to stop buying and selling links and try to remove those that already exist by contacting the sites and networks involved. You can also use the Disavow tool in Google Webmaster Tools to have the links discarded:
https://support.google.com/webmasters/answer/2648487?hl=en

Other SEO tricks

Google also penalizes sites that engage in other forms of deception like keyword stuffing and cloaking (detecting a search engine robot and showing it different, highly optimized content). If you have to think about whether something you're doing could be thought of as an attempt to trick search engines, it probably is and you should stop.

How to get your site back in Google

The first step is to fix all of the problems areas. Unless you do that, a re-inclusion request will fail.

Sending your request via Google Webmaster Tools will give you the best chance of success. List all the corrections you've made and be as detailed as you can. Once you've submitted your request you may need to wait weeks or even months for your site to be reinstated to the Google index.

Not every request is successful, so depending on the scale of the problem you might decide that starting from scratch is actually the less time-consuming option.

SEO Glossary - Key Terms Explained

Like most things connected with the web, SEO uses a lot of terms and abbreviations. Here are the most common terms you should be familiar with.

Anchor / link text
The words of an HTML link that form the linked text. For example, in the link wordpress themes, the anchor text is "wordpress themes".

AuthorRank
Similar to PageRank (see below), ranks content by the same author based on the popularity and authority of their previous published content.

Authority site
A site that has a number of links to it from well-established and important sites in the same niche, leading to a high trust factor and ultimately better search rankings.

Backlink
A link back to your site from another site that can be followed by search engines. A link in a blog post, a social network profile or on a forum are all examples of backlinks.

Black hat / white hat
Black hat SEO uses tricks to try and game search engines into giving high rankings by using loopholes and spamming tactics. White hat SEO uses the type of strategies covered in this book which follow Google's SEO guidelines.

CTR / Click-Through Rate
The percentage of people who click on a particular link, banner ad or other clickable element on a web page.

Crawling
When a search engine crawls your site, it moves slowly from one page to

another by following the links on the page. As it does, it collects data about the content of your page. Also called spidering.

External link
Any link that leads from one website to a different one.

GoogleBot
The name of the automatic crawler that indexes site for inclusion in Google. If you have access to statistics reports that use server log files, you may see visits listed as coming from GoogleBot.

Impressions
Often used in Google Analytics and Webmaster Tools reports, impressions means the number of times something has been seen. If a report says your site has 50,000 impression a month in Google search, it means your site appeared with search results 50,000 times that month.

Indexing
Once a search engine has crawled your site and has started to list it in search results, it's said to have indexed it.

Internal link
Any link that leads to another page on the same website.

Keywords
Any word or phrase used to search.

Keyword density
How many times a keyword appears in content, expressed as a percentage.

Keyword stuffing
The act of including many more mentions of a keyword than is natural in a page or post, in the hope of ranking better. Typical spamming technique, not recommended.

Landing page

In SEO terms, the first page a visitor arrives at when visiting your site from search engine results.

Linkbaiting
Publishing a controversial opinion - usually aimed at a popular blogger, company or celebrity - with the aim of generating a stink and a lot of links from outraged supporters.

Meta tags
HTML Tags that are placed within <head> part of a web page to give information about the page. For SEO purposes, there are three meta tags - title, description and keywords. The title tag is always used by search engines, the description is used sometimes. The keyword tag is no longer used by search engines and should be avoided.

PageRank
One of the many algorithms used by Google in search results. PageRank counts the number and quality of links to a page to give an estimate of how important the website is.

Traffic
Another word for visitors. Having a lot of traffic means having a lot of visitors.

SERPS
Short for Search Engine Results Pages, the pages that appear when you search for something.

robots.txt
The robots.txt file is a simple text file that tells search engines not to index certain files and folders on your server.

SEO Links and Resources

There are thousands of SEO-related blogs, sites and web apps out there. Here are the ones I recommend for providing updated, reliable information.

SEO Blogs

Moz
http://moz.com/blog
Ignore the weird name - this site is full of useful, actionable SEO-related tips.

Search Engine Land
http://searchengineland.com
Comprehensive coverage of search engines and everything related - including SEO, Local SEO and Social Media Marketing.

Search Engine Watch
http://searchenginewatch.com
Frequent updates on SEO, Google and Social Media marketing. Good place to learn about more advanced techniques now that you've read this book.

Google related

Algroo
http://algoroo.com/
Tracks changes in rankings for thousands of keywords to predict whether a Google algorithm change has taken place. The higher and redder the bar chart, the more likely there's been a change.

Google Analytics Dashboard Gallery
http://www.google.com/analytics/learn/solutions-gallery.html
Dashboards in Google Analytics are collections of data filters that help you see how well you're performing in areas like social media, search engine keyword optimization and ecommerce customer conversions.

The official Google SEO guidelines

http://support.google.com/webmasters/bin/answer.py?hl=en&answer=35769

If you've read this far, there's nothing new in these guidelines but it's always a good idea to keep an eye on what Google currently likes or doesn't like, along with the thinking behind algorithm updates.

Matt Cutts

http://www.mattcutts.com/blog/type/googleseo/

As head of Google's Anti-Webspam team, Matt Cutts posts regularly about updates Google makes to improve search results. His blog is a good way to understand how to keep on the good side of Google and read details about algorithm updates affecting rankings.

Free Keyword Tools

Keyword Spy

http://www.keywordspy.com

Probably the most used keyword tool out there. Normally a paid tool, but you can use the free 14-day trail period to uncover the best keywords for your niche.

WordTracker

https://freekeywords.wordtracker.com

Useful keyword information, including how much competition you're likely to face for a particular keyword - but you'll need to create an account to use it. You can get up to 50 keyword suggestions per search with a free account.

Thank you for reading

If you've enjoyed reading this book, please consider writing a quick review on the Amazon page for the book. It really helps to spread the word so that more people can start getting the traffic their site deserves. Here's the link:

http://www.amazon.com/dp/B00AAY00ZQ/

Need more help? Something you'd like to ask? Feel free to email me at the address below.

Best,
Caimin Jones
hello@geniusstartup.com

PS: Here's that link mentioned at the beginning of the book for the free, no-obligation two-week trial of the awesome SEMRush.com PRO SEO tool:

http://bit.ly/semrush-offer

38964239R00075

Made in the USA
Lexington, KY
31 January 2015